Tame That Stitch

Boone McReynolds

For

Barbara

Self Help

For

Your Sewing Machine

Forward

The purpose of this little piece is to aid the sewing person (that's you) in troubleshooting sewing problems without the help of a sewing machine technician.

And who am I to tell you this? That's a fair question.

I'm a retired mechanical engineer, who grew up professionally as a "mechanism designer," retiring in the late 1990's. Attended engineering classes with a slide rule on my belt, which gives one an idea of the time frame.

I started sewing (quilting, mostly) when my wife became unable to see and required assistance in her quilting activities. Pretty soon, I was doing all the sewing for her. She then fell victim to Alzheimer's and passed away several years ago, leaving me with some major medical expenses. And some spare time.

In order to solve those two problems, I went to work as a sewing machine technician, found I really liked it and, several years later, have actually become somewhat proficient at it.

The problem that keeps coming up in my work has to do with customers who have sewing issues and don't have access to a technician at the time of the event. Perhaps an issue that could have been solved or prevented at home.

We can help that!

I still want your business, but don't want you having difficulties that can be solved at home with your misbehaving sewing machine.

So...enjoy the book! I hope it helps.

Boone McReynolds....Pueblo, Colorado

Kindly Old Technician

Table of Contents

A Little History

Sometimes, it's easier to understand a problem, if you have at least a rudimentary understanding of the development history. The following is a VERY brief history of home sewing machine technology:

The earliest of the current machine types were end loading, straight-stitch designs. The hook/bobbin assembly was rotary, and mounted directly to the end of the main shaft. Very simple and straight-forward. A well known example is the Singer Featherweight, and the early treadle machines.

Almost from the very beginning, there was a desire for a "stretch" or zig-zag feature. This required moving the needle sideways, as well as feeding the fabric forward. The end loaders accomplished this by moving the entire hook, bobbin and needle assembly back and forth along the axis of the main shaft. Lots of design complication, extra parts, etc. needed to do this. The remedy for that was to move the hook/bobbin arrangement to the front of the machine. This allowed side movement of the needle with-out the cumbersome design of a zig-zag end loader. End loaders, however, did not die away completely, and are still available today, as a piecing/free motion machine. The modern end loader is an almost in-dustrial design, and very fast. Straight stitch only, but very capable.

With the advent of front loading machines, it was possible to accomplish not only zig-zag, but decora-tive stitches. At about the same time, top loaders came along, and enjoyed the same simplicity of design as front loaders. Most of the front loaders, by the way, were oscillating hook designs. In other words, the hook doesn't rotate all the way around, but drives just far enough to get the top thread around the bobbin, then comes back to rest position. Although somewhat controversial, there is a general industry opinion that the oscillating hook results in a superior stitch. I, personally, can see very little, if any dif-ference in stitch quality between top and front loaders. In order to accomplish a wider zig-zag or deco-rative stitch, the front loaders have been forced to use a full rotary hook, which is capable of wider nee-dle swings.

All of the zig-zag capable machines began with mechanical movement of the needle. Cams with spring-loaded cam followers, and spring-loaded cam selection mechanisms. The spring loaded stuff is im-portant to you as a user, because those mechanisms tend to "gum up" over time, and require frequent cleaning and lubricating. The number of cams that can be practically stacked up inside a machine also limits the number of decorative stitches available. Some machines feature removable cam stacks, to make a larger selection available. The selection, however, is still somewhat limited.

In the early 1970's, two events took place which had huge impacts on the modern sewing machine. And on the people who use them.

The first event was the widespread use of "self lubricating" bearings. People who manufactured and sold machines equipped with these bearings marketed them as never needing oil. Time has since proved that to be unrealistic. Not a good thing for the customer with a frozen bearing who was told, in all good faith at the time, that the new machine just purchased would never need service. The bearings in question are still in use, but now with regular cleaning and oiling widely accepted as being necessary. There was still the question of all the many small parts and assemblies within the machine that did not have the new bearings applied. The bearings, by the way, are sintered (pressed) iron, with graphite impregnated into them. When the upper hand wheel bearing seizes, the graphite shows up as black spots on the shaft near the bearing. Not a good thing! And expensive.

The second, and most important, major event was the introduction of an electrical device called a stepper motor. Stepper motors are very powerful motors, that, rather than rotating smoothly, rotate by small steps. They can be programmed to rotate to a given step position, and then lock at that position until commanded to move again. The commands for the motor movement come from a small computer chip located within the machine. The motors are extremely reliable. The "burp" you hear when you turn on a computer controlled machine, is the sound made by the step motors as they initialize.

The modern computer controlled machine is born!

The step motor revolution started with a stitch width (zig-zag) motor, and a feed motor. The feed motor is quite large compared to the needle motor, because it has to move more parts. Other motors were soon added. A step motor can be used to adjust tension for the stitch selected, move a scissor to cut threads, lift the presser foot, etc. Some machines have as many as 13 or 14 stepper motors.

The big deal, however, is that the number of decorative stitches now possible in a given machine is now almost limitless. Some machines offer over 1,000 different stitches, all selected from a chip about the size of a matchbook cover!

Since the electronics to control all those motors are now available, other functions can be easily added. Needle up/down, good speed control, touch screen user interfaces, etc.

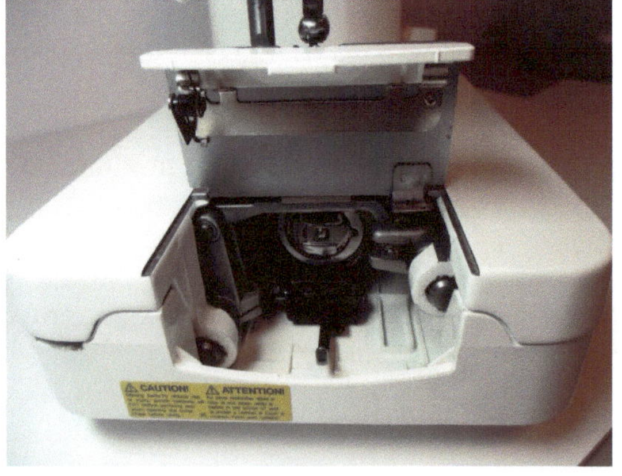

End Loader

Front Loader

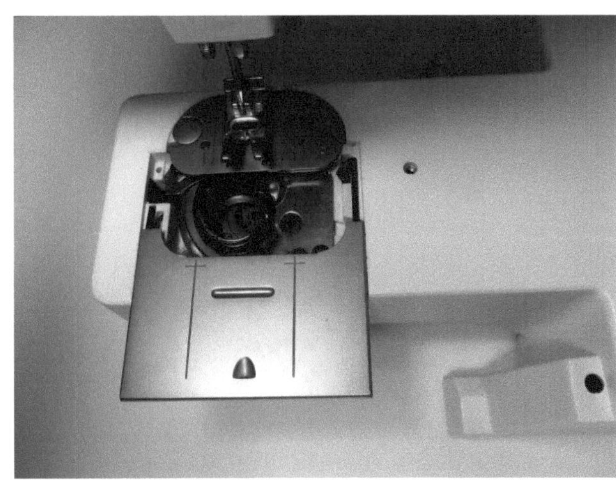

Step Motor

Top Loader

If you know just a bit about how your machine works, it'll make troubleshooting a lot easier.

Stitch Formation

OK..you now have some idea of what makes your machine go. But what happens when you step on the foot control and actually make stitches?

The answer is... lots of things happen!

The first thing that happens, is that the needle, with the top thread nestled in the eye, goes down and penetrates the fabric, taking the thread with it. As the needle starts back up, the thread gets wedged between the needle and the fabric, and a loop of thread bulges out from the back of the needle. We're still on the underside of the fabric. The hook we talked about earlier comes around just behind the needle, and catches the loop of thread and pulls it all the way around the bobbin. That can be around 4 inches of thread, depending on the machine and the stitch. As the needle rises above the fabric, the take up lever pulls up the extra thread that was wrapped around the bobbin case and pulls it back up, through the fabric and the needle, catching the bobbin thread as it does so, and creating a twist between the bobbin thread and the top thread. As this continues, a stitch is formed within the fabric. A small spring, called a "check spring" gives the stitch a final tug and tightens it.

Whew!! Got it? You don't have to understand this perfectly, that's my job, but having the general idea in mind will go a long way down the road of trouble shooting problems.

This seemingly complicated system has evolved through the years, and no one yet has found a simpler way to create a stitch.

For one thing, now you know that a bunch of thread gets dragged through the eye of the needle and the fabric, in both directions, every time you take a stitch. That's where all that lint comes from! It gets shaved off the thread at the needle eye. Some of the lint is from the fabric, but most comes from the thread.

Since we want the stitch to occur in the fabric, there's another component we need to talk about:

Tension

Virtually every machine that crosses my workbench exhibits a tension problem! It's the most common problem I see as a technician.

Think of tension as a tug-of-war. Top thread on one end of the rope, bottom thread on the other. Ideally, we want the crossover (the center of the rope in the tug-of-war) to occur within the fabric. That's what the pictures in your owner's manual and your machine screen show. As a practical matter, that's just not going to happen! Most of the fabric we deal with is as thin or thinner than the diameter of the thread. The mechanisms that control the tension are not as sensitive as we'd like them to be, so there are running variations in tension. Some of it in the thread itself, some in the thread delivery system, some in the tension mechanisms themselves. The best we can hope for is to show just a bit of top thread on the underside of the stitch, at each side of a zig-zag stitch. When you check your tension, use a zig-zag stitch because it makes it a lot easier to see what's going on. Check the back side of the stitch, with a contrasting color on the top and the bottom. As you can see in the picture, it's not perfect! To adjust the

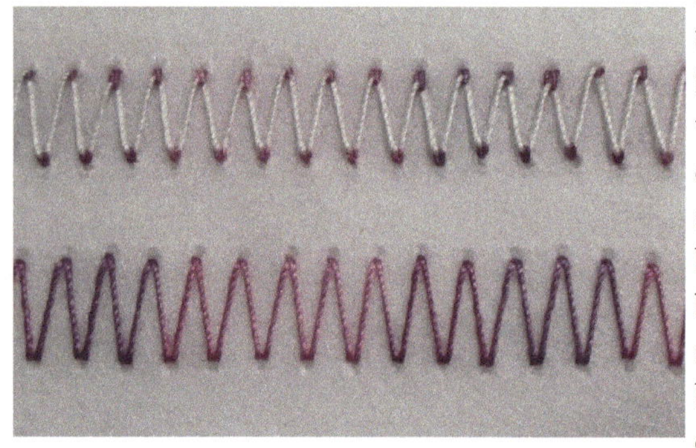

tension, remember the tug of war, and adjust the top tension to get the balance shown. If the bobbin tension is correct, or nearly so, then the top should be somewhere near the center of the range on the dial, usually 4 or 5. Or "Auto" if it's available. When I set your tension in the shop, I set the top at 4 or Auto and adjust the bobbin to get the correct pattern. A word on adjusting bobbin cases: a little goes a long way! The manuals all say to set the bobbin tension so that if you hold the bobbin case by the thread, the case should very slowly drop. Wrong!! That won't be enough bobbin tension. It also only applies to end or front loaders. When you make a change to the bobbin case tension, think of the screw that loads the flat tension spring as a clock face, and only move it one hour (5 minutes) at a time. Turning the screw clockwise will increase the bobbin tension and pull more top thread to the back. The same 5 minute rule applies to top loaders. If this is more than you want to handle, bring your tension problem to a technician, and let him (or her) mess it up! Just kidding, most technicians should be able to handle it without a problem. As an aside, top loaders will show more top thread on one side of the back of the zig-zag stitch than the other.

Remember to set your tension with the same weight and type of thread top and bottom. I see a fair amount of front loader bobbin cases with the tension screw way too loose. That probably happened "by itself," the screw just loosened up. The tension of the spring is supposed to keep the screw where it was put, but: .. sometimes. If the screw is way too tight, someone thought it was a fastening device, not an adjustment, and cranked it down.

Most machines control top tension by pulling the thread between two disks, which are spring loaded to squeeze the thread as it is pulled by.

On manual (non-computerized) machines you are increasing or decreasing the spring tension on the disks when you adjust the top tension. The higher the number, the more tension on the top thread.

If your machine is computerized, there are various levels of computer control involved. Generally, the newer and more complicated the machine, the more control the computer has over the tension. Earlier computerized machines will have an "Auto" position to enable the control. This is all because each different stitch has an optimum tension setting, painstakingly arrived at by testing of each of the possible selected stitches by the manufacturer. Quite an undertaking if the machine has hundreds of stitches available!

As I said earlier, when I set your tension in the shop, I set the dial at 4 or 5. If the machine has the "Auto" feature, that's the one I use. At least theoretically, that should optimize the tension for any stitch selected. On some computerized machines, the tension automatically selected by the machine when you pushed the button for that stitch will show up on the display. In that case, you can probably modify it somewhat by touching the tension symbol on the display, to set it higher or lower. If you don't put that modification in memory, your machine will revert back to the default setting when you shut it off and restart it.

One exception to the spring loaded tension disk design, in all it's various forms, is by a well-known Japanese manufacturer, who, on some of their products, has moved away from disks, and controls the thread tension by clamping the thread between two rollers and a rough-finished shaft on a small stepper motor. The step motor can then control the tension much more accurately than the disk method. It works quite well, with one notable exception: every time I get one of these machines in for service, there are large amounts of thread tangled up in the rollers, and the system doesn't work right as a result. That's a problem for you as a customer, because the motor-roller mechanism is buried inside the machine, requiring some disassembly to get at it to remove the thread.

If you have one of those, you can tell by turning on a threaded machine and pulling on the thread downstream of the tension unit, with the presser foot down. If the thread is clamped down tightly so that it breaks before moving when you pull on it, then it's one of these systems.

The cure is to be very careful when you thread the top thread through the tension unit, and have the machine serviced regularly. If you're experiencing tension problems that can't be adjusted out, then see your local technician.

When you're doing free motion, add a few points to the top tension setting; say from 4 to 6 or 8.

Whew! Lots of information! If it's too much information, just take from it what you can use, and don't worry about the rest. Tension issues are a major part of your life as a machine driver, though, so it's a good thing to be informed.

Timing

I'm sure you've all heard the term "out of time" many times, but what does it really mean? It refers to the relation of the hook to the needle position, and the needle position to the feed dogs. The feed dogs are the pointy things that rise up from the surface of the needle plate to drive your fabric. Now you've learned a new engineering term: "pointy things!"

First of all, the feed dogs need to lower themselves below the top of the needle plate before the needle descends into the fabric. We don't want to be feeding the fabric while the needle is embedded in it!

Next, the hook should pass by the back of the needle in such a manner that, at the far extreme of the needle travel sideways, the hook is just at the top of the eye of the needle as it passes the needle. The needle is starting to go up at this point, so this is a bit touchy. If this condition isn't met, stitches will be missed, because the hook will not be able to catch the loop of thread at the back of the needle. If the hook passes by the needle either too high or too low, stitches will be dropped.

OK...you're saying, "What does this have to do with me?" The answer is simple; if you see the needle in the fabric when the fabric is still feeding, or if stitches are being skipped on a wide zig-zag or deco stitch, your machine must be brought in to a technician. With one exception...see below.

Needle not all the way up is sometimes called "False timing." That one you can fix yourself!

Machines have timing issues for one of three reasons, in my experience.

First: Parts are worn so that the hook gets to the needle too late.

Second: Something has slipped out of adjustment.

Third: Someone has moved an adjustment out of its proper place. (Your husband?)

There are some other reasons stitches can be skipped; the hook passes by the needle too far away from the needle, in which case, see your local technician, or the needle is not all the way up in the clamp.

My point here is that if it really is out of time, don't keep fighting it and getting frustrated, because this is something you probably can't fix at home. Unless the needle isn't in all the way, so check that before you pack it up and carry it to the shop.

Timing isn't a common problem. I probably see it in one out of 30 or 40 machines. Maybe less than that. Of the three causes above, worn parts are the most common reason.

One other point: Timing is (or should be) checked at each annual service. I don't charge extra for adjusting it at a service job, but some technicians may.

Threading

Threading, especially the upper thread, seems to be a problem for new users and occasionally for old hands that have done it a million times. Or maybe you're at a quilt retreat and either you or the person next to you has a machine you're just not familiar with. For whatever reason this may come up...there's a rule. There are a large number of different machines with different thread paths, but the rule still holds!

Here it is: The top thread on virtually all machines will take the same path, although it may look very different. The thread will come off the spool either from the end of the spool or the side of the spool. From there, it will go in to one or sometimes two pre-tensioners. Their purpose is to get the thread under control and smooth out twists and tangles. (within reason) From there it will go into the top tension unit. That will be somewhere in the vicinity of where you might expect it, but it's always the next point. Next will be a little spring with a protruding arm. The check spring. It may be built into the tension unit or be a separate entity. It's got to be there, or the stitch quality will suffer. Next in line is the take-up lever. On some machines, it will be hidden and the thread will go into it automatically. Trust me here; it's in there. Next is either a thread guide or sometimes just a wear strip. And lastly, a small guide located on the needle clamp. Then, of course, the needle itself.

Got it? Spool, pre-tensioner, tension unit, check spring, take-up lever, lower thread guide, (or strip) needle clamp guide and the needle.

So, let's talk a bit about all these various elements and how they affect your sewing life. There are only two ways to get thread off the spool and into your machine. Both have good and bad points. If the thread comes off the side of the spool, with the spool vertical, it will not be prone to tangling, because it doesn't get twisted as it comes off, but the spool tends to over-run and then jerk the thread when it tightens up again. That has a direct effect on top tension. In my opinion, however, this is the most trouble free of the two methods, although manufacturers are moving away from it, I believe because of a perceived styling issue.

In most newer machines, the thread comes off the end of the spool, which can be either vertical or horizontal. In either orientation, the thread gets twisted as it comes off the spool. The finer the thread, the more that becomes an issue. Embroidery machines are affected more than sewing machines, partly because of the use of finer thread. If you are having issues with thread tangling up before it gets into the tension unit, it will show up as a tension problem, a thread breaking problem, or a needle breaking problem. That's because the thread tangled itself into a knot that got wedged at the pre-tensioner. The cure is to use a thread net around the spool, or a thread stand behind the machine.

Speaking of pre-tensioners, most of them use a very light spring loaded plate to smooth out the thread. The Japanese like to use a blade with (usually) 3 smooth holes in it. The thread goes in one hole, around the blade, through another hole, and in to the tension unit. Be careful with this; it's easy to get the thread wrapped around the end of the blade, where it will essentially tie itself into a knot. Sergers almost all universally use a blade for a pre-tensioner. The good news is: if you get the thread past the pre-tensioner without mishap, then you're pretty much home free!

Another point about threading the top thread: always get the thread past the tension unit with the presser foot in the raised position. That's because raising the presser foot releases the tension, and allows the thread to snuggle in between the tension disks. It's OK to lower the foot after the thread is seated between the disks. That makes threading the needle a bit easier. The majority of Sergers don't release the tension when the foot is raised, so give each thread a tug to seat it in it's respective tension unit when you thread it. Threading Sergers is a whole different world, by the way, and we'll address that later on.

Be careful when you finish all this threading and flip the thread back under the presser foot, not to twist the thread around the needle. I see this often enough to warrant a word. (or two) Also, remember, if you have an end loader, the thread goes into the needle from the grooved side to the flat side.

Did you know that bobbins have a right side and a wrong side? They do! Even if the bobbin itself is symmetrical, the way the thread is wound around it makes it asymmetrical. On an end loader or a front loader, you have the bobbin case in your hand, looking at the back side, when you insert the loaded bobbin. The bobbin thread should come off the right-hand side of the bobbin. After threading, the bobbin should turn clockwise when you pull on the thread. We're still looking at the back of the bobbin case. If it doesn't, just flip the bobbin over and re-insert it into the case.

Top loaders are different, in that the bobbin thread should come off the left-hand side. If it isn't doing that, just flip it over. Most top loaders have a little picture on the bobbin case cover plate showing this.

If the bobbin is in upside down, you will have all sorts of problems, so it's worth paying attention to.

If, for any reason, the thread is not in the take-up lever, serious looping on the underside of the stitch will be present. That's all that thread we talked about earlier that the take-up lever is supposed to handle. Whether you missed the take-up lever when you threaded the machine, or it slipped out while you were sewing, rethread the top thread all the way from the spool to the needle.

Looping on the back side of the stitch can be caused by other things, such as a piece of thread caught in either the top or bobbin case tension unit. If it's the top tension, there is a special tool to get it out. It's a specialized tool called a pipe cleaner. For the bobbin case, the specialized tool is the corner of an index card or business card. Carefully swiped in between the tension spring and the side of the bobbin case.

Might save you a trip to the shop.

When you have a problem, always try re-threading before you panic. It's a little like re-booting your computer. Sometimes it actually works.

Needles

Needles, of course, are more complicated than one would think. I'm not going to get into which needle to use for each sewing condition; there are reams of information on that already out in the world. There are some things that will give you problems, however, and we can talk about those now.

Virtually all home sewing machines use the same type of needle. That is: 130/705 H. 130 is the length, 705 means it has a flat shank, H means it has a scarf. By flat shank, we mean the flat on the back of the needle body that goes into the needle clamp. If you look at the end that goes up in the machine, it looks like the letter "D". Newer machines have a D shaped hole, so you can't install the needle incorrectly. Backwards, in other words. Older machines sometimes have a round hole, so be careful to get the needle in with the flat to the back. I should really say, with the flat towards the hook. That's important if you have an end loader machine. Some have the hook outboard of the needle, some inboard, so be careful! The "scarf" refers to a sort of groove in the back of the needle. Virtually all needles sold today have this feature. It allows the hook to get closer to the axis of the needle, for fewer skipped stitches. The front of the needle has a groove running down the front, from the top of the needle to the eye. That groove size is proportional to the diameter of the needle. The thread lays in that groove, and should not be too tight or too loose. If the thread is too large for the groove, it will break often. That condition is called "stifling." If it is too small for the groove, stitches may be missed. That's because the loop we referred to earlier won't be properly formed, and the hook may miss it. Good quality thread will tell you on the label what size needle to use with that particular thread.

The needle size is the diameter of the body of the needle. This gets a little confusing here, because there are two different systems for identifying size! European systems have the last number in the needle code referring to the diameter in millimeters. A #70 needle is 0.7 mm, a #90 is 0.9mm, etc. Corresponding American sizes are shown in the chart. In both cases, the larger the number, the bigger the needle. As you would expect, the size of the needle eye will change as the diameter of the needle changes. The size of the eye also changes with the type of needle. A topstitch needle has a larger eye than a universal needle of the same size, for instance. Generally, embroidery thread is quite well suited for a size 10 or 11 needle. piecing thread, a size 11 or 12, and quilting thread a size 12 or 14. Thread sizes, of course, have their own numbering system, and we'll take up that challenge when we get to the thread discussion. Keep in mind, also, that if you use the needle threader built into most new machines, it should not be used with a needle smaller than a #11. The tiny hook that goes through the needle eye will be damaged if the eye is too small, and you will have to have the threader head replaced. Before you engage the needle threader, make sure the needle is in the up position, to avoid damaging the little hook. Change your needle often. When you remove a used needle, discard it. If you put it back in the little container, it will look just like a new one.

Sewing Machine Needle Sizes	
American	European
8	60
9	65
10	70
11	75
12	80
14	90
16	100
18	110

Thread

You probably already know that thread has a twist. It's like a small rope. The fibers are woven into strands, which are then twisted together to form the thread itself. What you may not know about thread twist, is that there are two different types. Z twist and S twist. The type you want in your sewing machine is Z twist. If you hold a cut piece of thread in your hand and look at the end, the twist should be counter-clockwise. If you twist that piece of thread counter clockwise, it should tighten. As shown in the little picture. Some of the "dual purpose" thread on the market is S twist, which may account for some of the problems we encounter with it. You should always check this when you buy a new brand of thread.

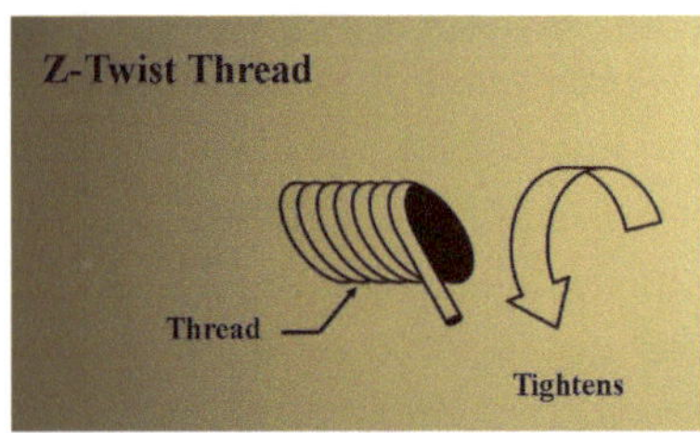

Do you have a bunch of Grandma's heirloom thread in your stash? Before you use it, you should know that thread has a shelf life. The length of that life depends on when the thread was manufactured. And what it's made of. Cotton thread made 15 or 20 years (or more) ago should not be used. If it's newer than that, it's probably OK to use. Polyester thread is forever, so don't worry about that. Other plastic threads, such as rayon or acrylic, have a good shelf life, but a lot of sewing machines don't do well with those materials.

When you buy cotton thread, look for the words "long staple" on the label. That product will sew better and produce less lint. That will make your machine last longer and your service technician won't need a shovel to remove all that lint! Lint is abrasive, and is attracted to oil and grease, which means it will find it's way to the parts of your machine where it can do the most harm.

A quick note: When you clean out your machine, the bobbin area is about the only place you can get to. Always use a small brush, like a mascara brush, (a new one) and a vacuum cleaner with a small tip. If you blow the lint away, it will end up further inside your machine, where it will not be welcome. No canned air, in other words!

Thread sizes are somewhat confusing, but keep in mind that the higher the number, the smaller the diameter. #100 is extremely fine, #60 is most embroidery threads, #50 is piecing and general sewing, # 40 is what's normally used for quilting. Heavier threads will be for heavy denim, canvas, etc.

Monofilament thread, sometimes called invisible thread, is a single strand of plastic. It looks like fishing line, and in fact is manufactured by fishing line companies. When monofilament is used as a top thread, #60 weight bobbin thread will be the most compatible. Keep in mind that most machines use plastic in parts that are in contact with the thread, and monofilament thread will wear grooves in those parts at a much higher rate than regular thread. Your service technician may have to replace those parts at your regular service appointment.

One last point about thread...don't use serger thread in your sewing machine; it's not as strong, has different tension characteristics, and will generate lots of extra lint. Stitches may be skipped.

Satin Stitch

Sometimes called "satin stitch blues." The problem most people have with satin stitches are jamming the stitch down into the needle plate and not then being able to feed the material.

First of all, check the presser foot. It should have a rather large groove, or relieved area, on it's underside, which gives the stitch a place to go instead of trying to cram itself into the needle plate. The correct foot will help more than anything else you can do.

Other remedies are keeping presser foot pressure as high as possible and opening up the stitch length a bit. Most satin stitch default machine settings for stitch length are 0.4 millimeters. If the thread is heavy, opening this up to 0.5 or 0.6 will probably help, without cosmetic degradation. The machine doesn't know what size thread you put in it, so the default setting may not be correct. Imagine a flat bed truck with a load of pipe stacked one layer high. The smaller the pipe, the closer they can be to each other. And vice-versa.

Bobbins

We talked about bobbins being in upside down, but not about the various types. This is another irrelevant system of classification, but it's what we've got.

Plastic or metal? Your top loader machine probably has a magnetic bobbin system, and should use a plastic bobbin, which is non-magnetic. Makes sense to me. OK....A metal bobbin will suck up the magnetic forces which are intended to keep the bobbin case under control. So plastic does make sense. Plastic, if it's the right size, will work almost everywhere, and will be quieter and smoother than metal.

There are 5 basic sizes of bobbins in use by home sewing machines today. They are:

Class 15, in either plastic or metal. The most common size. Plastic works well in all types of machines.
Class 66, which is used mostly in earlier Singer machines. Plastic or metal, somewhat domed on top and bottom.
Class L, which is slightly lower in height than a class 15. Plastic or metal. Some L bobbin machines use a light beam to determine bobbin fill, and they must use the manufacturers bobbin.
Class M, which is mostly used in industrial machines, but occasionally appears in home machines.
Class "Other," which are special bobbins used by specific machines. Mostly by European makes.

Bobbin wound without tension. The bobbin winding tension unit was missed when the bobbin winding threading was done.

Cleaning, Lubrication

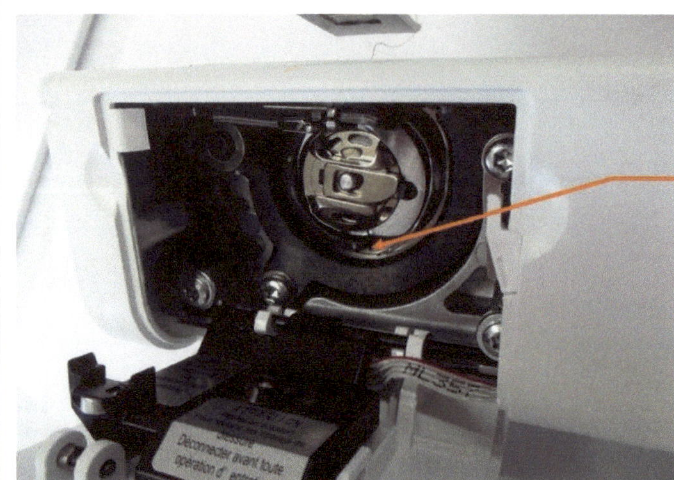

Front Loader with Rotary Hook

Just an occasional drop on the hook surface that rotates inside the black ring.

The places that are accessible to the user for lubrication are somewhat limited. The newer the machine, the more limited they are. The pictures show the oiling points that are available to the user of a later model machine.

Front Loader with Oscillating Hook

Oil here.

A drop in the groove behind the hook, about every 6 or 8 bobbins. And on the black plastic gate (or metal ring) covering the hook. If you wait too long, your machine will remind you by making unpleasant noises. It's called "hook clatter."

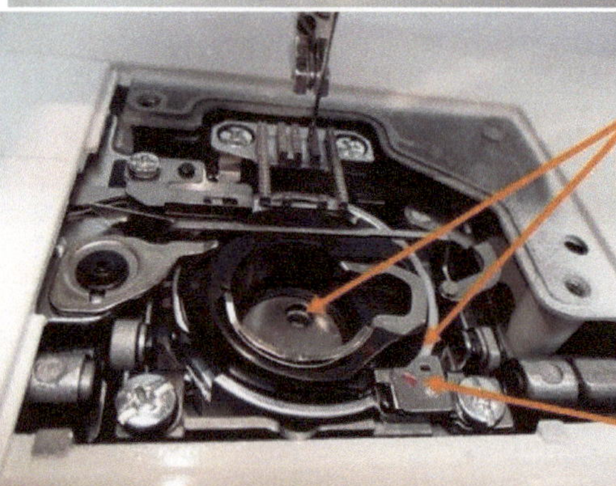

Top Loader.

Oil here.

A drop every 10 to 12 bobbins in the center hole, under the bobbin case. The hole has a wick in it, so don't pull it out thinking it's a gob of lint.

Also a drop on the outside of the hook, where the hook turns inside the bobbin case. Make sure the arrows are lined up.

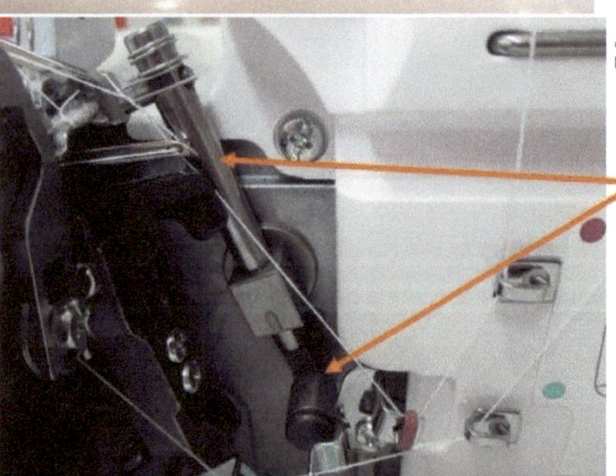

Serger.

-12-

Oil here. Just a drop on the rod, and the pivot point, after each project.

If your machine is older, and you know where the oiling points are and how to get to them, go ahead and oil them. For most points, once a year will do it. Use a high quality machine oil. Don't use WD-40 or 3-in-1 oil. The oil should be clear, and about the consistency of 5 weight motor oil. For newer machines, the oiling points are well hidden, and require major disassembling of the machine to get access.

Annual Machine Service

Ever wonder what happens at your annual service visit? Besides the charge? When you bring your machine in for service, make sure the technician knows what, if any, issues you may be having. They will then get special attention. Your machine will be stripped down to what is called the "skeleton." All the covers will be removed, and major sub-assemblies are also removed. Hooks, scissor mechanisms, etc. All parts, including the covers, inside and outside, are cleaned. Assemblies are lubricated and adjusted as needed. Generally speaking, everything that moves will be examined and adjusted and lubricated. Your machine will then be re-assembled, and tested using a standard thread set. Also your own thread, if you asked earlier and brought it with you. Computer chips will be updated, if the manufacturer has provided the update. The technician will go down a long list of tests to make certain that everything works as designed. This process takes about 2 to 3 hours for a regular sewing machine. Longer if it includes embroidery, or is especially complicated. (that's how long it takes me. I suspect that other technicians will take just as long, at least I hope so) Before you bring in your machine, make sure that everything the technician needs to sew a zig-zag stitch is with it. If embroidery is involved, a small hoop and the embroidery foot, also. If you're having an issue with free motion, make sure the darning foot is with the machine.

Yes; real technicians do free motion!

Skeletons in the Closet!   **Yuk!**

-13

-

"It Won't Run!"

If it just won't go, or the display won't light up, there are some obvious things to check. Is there electricity at the plug in the wall, and is the machine plugged in to it? I know, but check it, anyway. Did it stop when you were sewing, or when you came back from vacation? If it stopped while you were sewing, was there an event, such as a stalled motor involved?

OK, I'm not trying to be smart here, but sometimes the simplest things get us frustrated. If the display doesn't light up, for instance, did the contrast dial get bumped? That happens on machines with a little wheel or dial on the outside of the machine to adjust the contrast. If the machine stalled due to a heavy load, a fuse is most likely the culprit. A fuse will require a visit to the shop for most machines. The fuse will be buried deep inside, where a technician has to go. It's actually a rare event.

If the machine lights up, and the motors burp when it's turned on, etc., then maybe the foot control isn't plugged in, or the wire is damaged, if it still won't run.

On one nameless brand of European machine, if the machine sits idle for some time, nothing will happen when the power is turned on, because a capacitor in the power supply circuit board has discharged. In that case, turning on the power and waiting, sometimes for over an hour, will fix it. Beats replacing the power supply! It only happens after an extended off time, usually several weeks, or months. And not every time.

Whenever something like this happens, ask yourself "What did I do just before this happened?"

And, I have to ask…"Did your husband work on it?" Sometimes, I get a box of loose parts to put back together after a spouse attempted a repair.

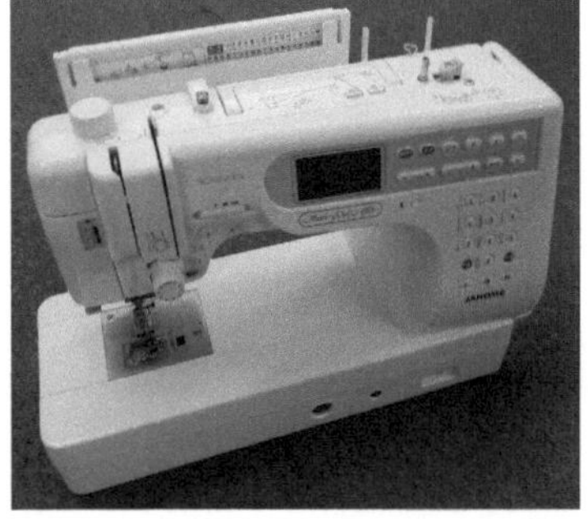

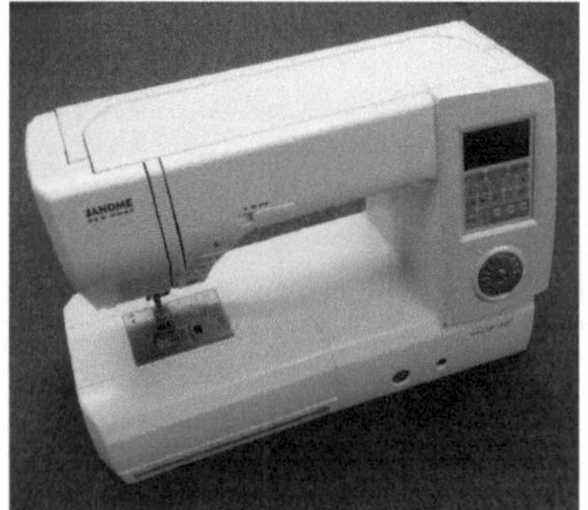

Sergers

Sergers are a bit more complicated mechanically than a sewing machine, and I think a lot of people are somewhat intimidated by the mechanical maze they present.
The complaint we hear the most, of course, is that they're hard to thread. That's somewhat true, but it can be optimized if you're careful about a few things.

First: Thread the upper looper first, followed by the lower looper. That usually means you start at the second position in from the right, followed by the first. If you don't follow this rule, the lower looper thread will break often, and you'll become a bit frustrated. Most threading diagrams tell you this, but in a subtle way that you may miss.
By the way, if you bring your machine in for service, bring the thread with it, and you'll get your machine back threaded.
Also keep in mind that sergers need service more often than sewing machines, so if you use yours fairly often, bring it in more often for cleaning and oiling. Remembering all those parts!
And the fact that sergers are the lint-making champions of the sewing world!

Second: When you thread the lower looper, the one everyone has trouble with, be very careful to run the thread through each and every guide. That goes for all the threads at every position, but the lower looper is the one people mess up the most often. Open the side door to get to the entry point of the looper, and rotate the handwheel to get access to both ends of the looper. A small crochet hook and a good pair of tweezers will help here. And maybe a magnifying glass. And a small flashlight. Prayer is optional.

Third: Use the correct needles. Most sergers use the same needles your regular sewing machine uses, but not all. If in doubt, check the book. We always change the needles at a service, and have found that bigger is better. That just means use #14 needles instead of embroidery needles. That's because there is a lot more pressure from thread pushing sideways against the needle in a serger than in a sewing machine.
One more note on needles. They each go in at a different height, so don't worry about them being uneven, just make sure they're in completely.

Fourth: When you complete threading, don't run the machine initially without fabric in it. Once it's sewed on fabric, it can make a "chain", and the start-up is easy. Always let it make a couple of inches of chain after you complete a seam, before you cut the thread, leaving the chain in the machine for the next seam.

Fifth: Make sure the thread is all the way into the tension disks when you thread the machine initially. Most sergers don't release the tension when the foot is raised, so give the thread a tug to seat it in the disks.

Serger Timing

First off, let me say that sergers are very seldom out of time; it's something that a lot of people worry about, however, so here's a little information to let you self-diagnose if yours is actually out of time. The most common reason for timing errors is human; the wrong person worked on the machine. Machine wear is a remote possibility.

First, rotate the hand wheel (in the proper direction; some sergers run "backwards", so look at the cover behind the hand wheel and check the graphic that tells you which way is forward) and turn the wheel until the needles are at top dead center. At that point, the eye of the upper looper should be centered in between the two needles. If your machine has only one needle, the eye should be right at the center of the needle.

Next, check to see if the lower looper tip is approximately 18.5 mm to the right of the stitch finger, when it's at the far right of it's travel.

OK so far?

One more thing to check, if the above looks OK.

Rotate the hand wheel some more, until the upper looper passes behind the lower looper. You will see a relief on the back of the lower looper, and you want to check the clearance between the two loopers as they pass each other at that relief. The pass should be an "air kiss" with the smallest clearance possible without the loopers actually touching. This isn't really a timing check, but is most commonly thought to be a timing error if it's not correct. It's a much more common problem, so check it while you're checking the timing.

If it all looks OK, and it still won't sew, check the threading and change the needles. The needles are much more critical in a serger than in a regular sewing machine. And remember; some sergers use different needles than your regular sewing machine. There will be a graphic on the machine if they should be different, telling you what they should be.

And...you know what to do if it still won't sew! See your local technician; repairing this is probably not something you want to tackle at home.

Needle Threaders

Most of the new machines incorporate a gadget called an "automatic needle threader." They're basically all the same device, some with some extra window dressing. And some with a <u>lot</u> of extra window dressing! They work by swinging a tiny little metal hook into the needle eye from the back of the needle. As the hook retracts, it pulls a loop of thread through the needle eye. As you can well imagine, that hook is really tiny, and rather delicate.

The problems I see with these devices in the shop are that the little hook is missing the needle eye, or it's been damaged. Another problem shows up in the fancier versions that incorporate a mechanism for presenting the thread to the threader. Sometimes the presentation doesn't present properly. That's annoying to you, (and to me) because it's usually difficult to manually present the thread when that part doesn't work correctly.

In any case, you probably have to bring your machine to the shop for a technician to repair. The parts are just too small to deal with at home. Your local technician will have small lights, magnifiers, etc. to deal with the repair. If you leave the shop after dropping off your machine, you won't hear the cussing and swearing from the back room.

While you're waiting to bring your machine in for this repair, try this little trick: When you must thread manually, snip off the end of the thread cleanly, and then, at an angle from slightly above, slide the cut end down the groove in the front of the needle. When the end of the thread gets to the eye of the needle, it'll go right in! Well...most of the time.

Another hint: When you use the machine's built-in needle threader, after it's threaded the needle, a few inches of thread are left hanging out of the needle. The hint is for you not to be tempted to save that "wasted" thread by pulling it backwards at the spool to save it. The needle threader will quite often damage the thread where the little hook pulls it through the needle, and you don't want that damaged section of thread to be sewn into your project. And you shouldn't pull the thread backwards, anyway.

I've mentioned elsewhere that engaging the threader with too small a needle, or engaging it when the needle is not all the way at the top will damage the threader.

Top Loader Bobbin Case

Top loader bobbin cases can rotate counter-clockwise past the bobbin stop. Or maybe someone installed them that way? If you attempt to sew when the case has rotated past it's stop, the bobbin case will be severely damaged. And your machine won't sew. This can happen if the little "stop nub" protruding from the side of the bobbin case gets worn or damaged, or if the stop is incorrectly adjusted. If you suddenly experience a problem with a top loader, check to see if this is the cause. If you didn't try to sew with it that way, re-installing it may save you a trip to the shop. If the stop is out of adjustment, or the bobbin case needs replacement, a technician should be involved in the repair.

The top loader bobbin case actually has two stops, the one that stops it from turning counter-clockwise, and a fixed stop across from that stop that prevents the case from "backing up" by turning clock-wise. It's trapped between the two stops. There has to be a gap between the stop nub on the case and the primary stop, because the thread must go by there. On most top loaders, the anti-backup stop is not a problem, but on some, the stop is located on the underside of the needle plate. If you have one of those, make sure the bobbin case is rotated counter-clockwise all the way when you install the needle plate. After cleaning out the bobbin area, for instance.

End and front loaders also have these stops, but because of their geometry, they are pretty much locked in, and inadvertent rotating isn't a problem. Be careful if you have a Singer Featherweight, because both the stops are located on the underside of the needle plate. The bobbin case has an ear that goes in between the two stops.

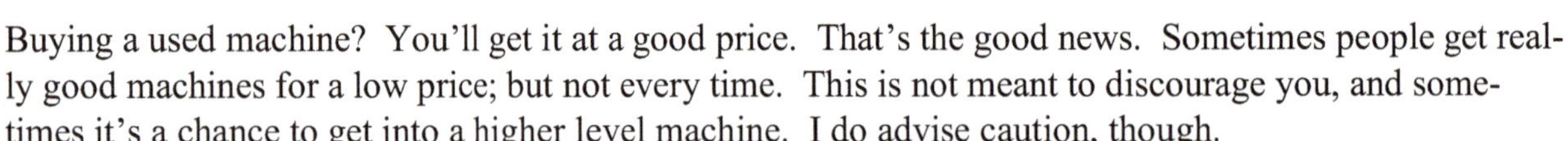

Used Machines

Buying a used machine? You'll get it at a good price. That's the good news. Sometimes people get really good machines for a low price; but not every time. This is not meant to discourage you, and sometimes it's a chance to get into a higher level machine. I do advise caution, though.

If you can make the deal such that the machine can be returned after a short grace period, that will be helpful, should you get an unpleasant surprise. It will also give you an opportunity to have a technician look over the purchase. Most technicians will give a used machine a check-up for a reasonable charge. That doesn't guarantee success, but a knowledgeable third party opinion can't hurt. Also, make sure that everything that should be there is, indeed, present. That's accessories, such as feet, extra bobbin cases, etc. A cord and foot pedal, for sure.

One thing you're probably not going to get, are lessons on the use of that machine. If you purchase your machine new, a reputable dealer will include lessons as part of the sale. Something to think about.

Also, keep in mind that some, but not all, top of the line machines have a stitch counter built into the machine. You will need a technician to look up that information. It's hidden inside where only technicians can go. Most good quality machines have a service life of 25 to 30 million stitches. If they've had good care, regular service, etc. Stitch counters are like the odometer in your car, in that they only count; they don't take harsh conditions into account, but they're still helpful information.

One other point: Check on the internet to see what others are paying for the machine you're considering. And happy shopping!

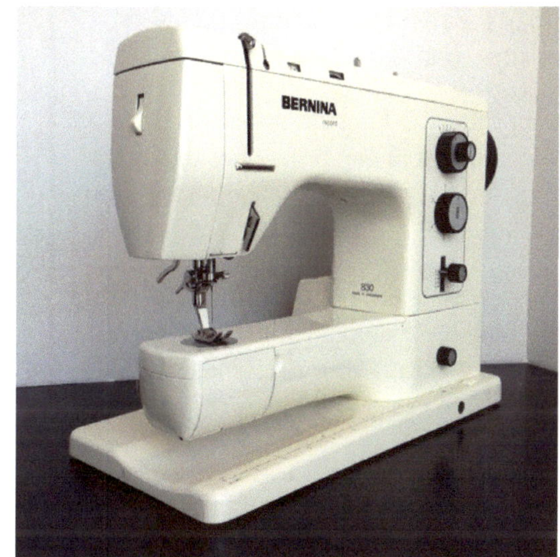

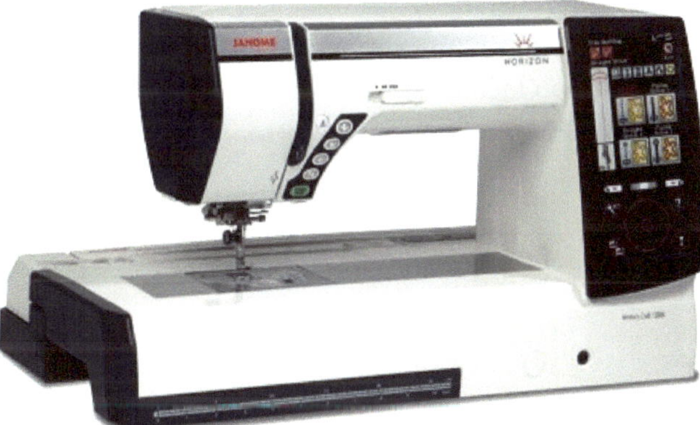

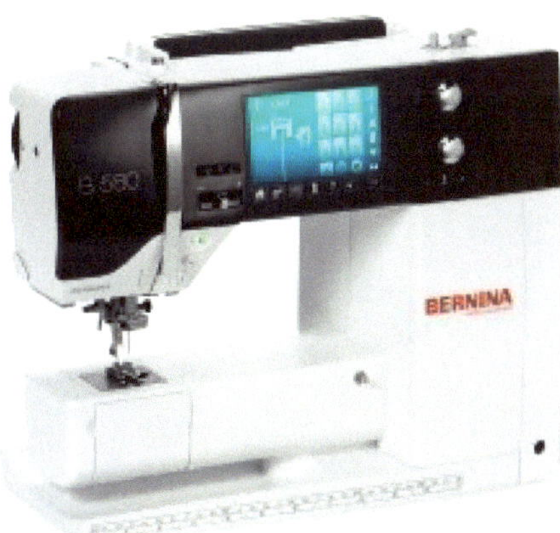

Feeding the Fabric

If you're like most of us, you don't think much about presser foot problems. One of the problems I see in the shop is a presser foot that's either sticky, or frozen. That's simply a result of deferred service. The presser foot rod needs cleaning and oiling. You can check this yourself by watching the presser foot when you drop it down. It should drop quickly, more or less as fast as your hand moves on the lever. If it doesn't move at all, or is obviously slow, it needs service.

Another culprit here is the feed dogs are not coming up high enough above the surface of the needle plate. If you watch closely, you should see them rise up about 1/32nd of an inch. That's just an approximation to assist you in diagnosis. Your technician uses a gauge to measure the actual height of the feed dogs above the needle plate. When you check this, make sure the feed dogs are at their topmost position, by turning the hand wheel and observing. If they aren't raising high enough, the repair must be done by a technician. The usual reason for this problem is worn parts; either the feed dogs themselves, or the mechanism that drives them up. Sometimes an adjustment slips, but that's fairly rare.

One other thing to check: Are the feed dogs simply in the dropped position? I get calls about this fairly often. If they just don't move up at all, this may be the culprit. Before you panic, remember that after they've been dropped, either manually or automatically by the machine, they won't come up until the machine has rotated through one cycle. One stitch, in other words.

While we're on the subject of feed dogs, I should mention that all feed dogs are not created equal. Some are made of soft (relatively) material, and will wear faster. Others may have an inadequate number of teeth. You can't do anything about the number of tooth sets, it's designed into your machine, but it's something to keep in mind for your next machine. I've seen as few as two sets, and as many as seven in different machines.

I see machines with a loose shank fairly often, so it's worth a mention. Keep that screw tight!

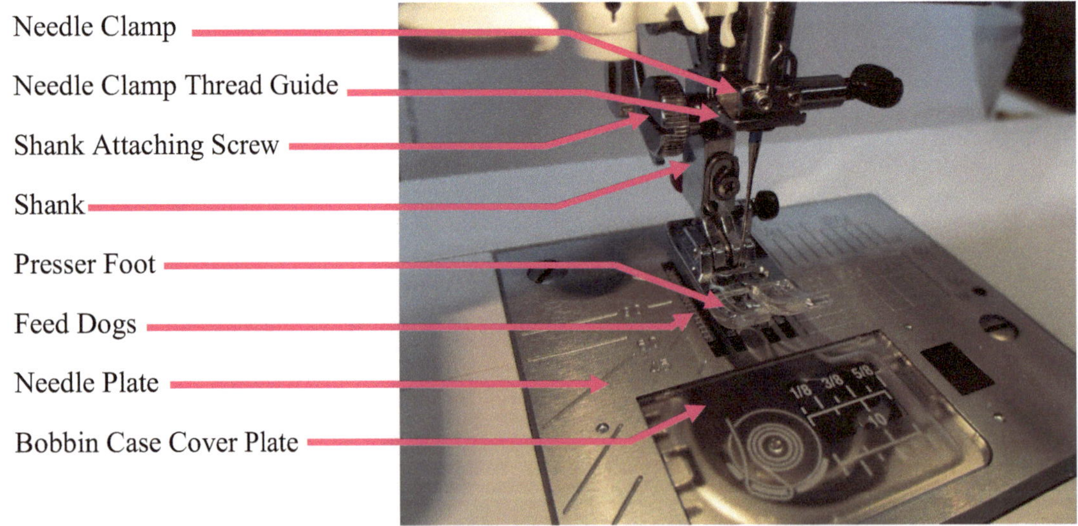

Error Messages

Computerized machines have an ability that we sometimes don't appreciate: they generate error messages! And, like your home computer, the error message doesn't always describe the error it's informing you of. If the message is a specific message, such as "error 3," consult your owner's manual for what that error means. The most annoying error message is one that just says "error" and won't let you do anything until whatever the problem is gets resolved. You may need a technician's help with that, but before you drag the beast into the shop, ask yourself what event may have just happened to cause the error. Maybe you can diagnose it yourself.

There are a couple of these messages you can deal with, however. If your machine tells you the top thread is broken, and it isn't, re-thread and try again. Most computerized machines use the motion of the check spring to signal a thread break. If the signal from the check spring is a light beam, dirt and lint are a possibility. Cleaning that out is best done in the shop, and is part of regular service. The check spring may be broken, but that's a very rare thing. If you can locate the sensor, which will be near the check spring, you may be able to clean it, but keep in mind that the parts are small and somewhat delicate, and be careful.

The message that tells you the bobbin is out of thread, or is about to be, is sometimes, but not always, generated by a light beam. Which is susceptible to dirt and lint, and is in a spot that will have plenty of both. You can usually find the light source and reflector and clean it at home. Be sure to clean both the light source and reflector. Bernina uses a light beam with their rotary hook machines that requires a clear path through the bobbin case front wall. Inside the bobbin case resides a flat, sort of conical spring, a "backlash" spring, which has a sight hole that must be matched up with the hole in the bobbin case, to let the light beam through. If your machine is continually telling you it's out of bobbin thread, and it isn't, check to see if the little spring is installed correctly. Designers use a light beam here, because the thread would interfere with a mechanical sensor if dynamic sensing is desired. Some manufacturers sense bobbin fill mechanically each time you start to sew, before the bobbin rotates. A snapshot, in other words. Less likely to be a problem, but the system isn't dynamic.

Anti-Backlash Spring

Raised Center Part of Spring.

Sight Hole.

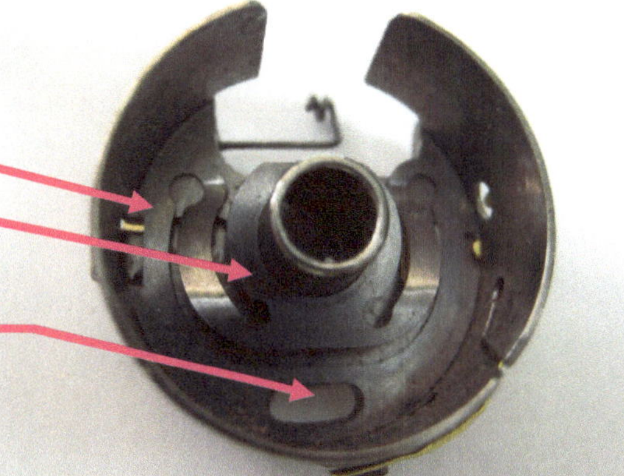

Power Transmission

OK...We have to get power (torque, which is twisting force) from the main motor to the moving parts of the machine. Most of the time, the motor will have a drive belt, either toothed or "V" shaped, which will turn the upper shaft. Sometimes there are two belts, and an idler pulley. Sometimes the motor drives the upper shaft with gears, avoiding the belt (s) entirely. The upper shaft has several jobs, but most importantly, it drives the needle and the take-up mechanism. At the driven (motor) end will be the hand wheel, and sometimes, but not always, the bobbin winder mechanism. The bobbin winder can also be driven by its own motor, or by the rotary hook, in the case of old Singers. Some older power transmission designs used a friction drive from the motor to the upper shaft. Thankfully, they did not persist, and are quite rare. An effort to reduce both cost and noise, I suspect.

The upper shaft drives the lower shaft either by a timing belt, or a vertical shaft with bevel gears. Most modern machines use a timing belt, because it's an efficient and cost saving method. The lower shaft drives the hook, and the feed system. Sometimes the scissor feature, but not always.

There are lots of transmission systems out there, as you can see. They all pretty much do the job, with an occasional broken belt to deal with. Motor belts are the ones that break, timing belts almost never. If you have a broken motor belt, you may be able to change and adjust it at home, but some cover removal will be necessary, and probably a belt tension adjustment. If your machine is _really_ old, the drive belts may be exposed and accessible, along with the belt tension adjustment. Belts should be loose enough not to put a big load on bearings, but tight enough to drive the mechanism without slipping.

The other comment on drive systems, is that they all generate noise, at least to some degree. Correct belt tension may help in that department.

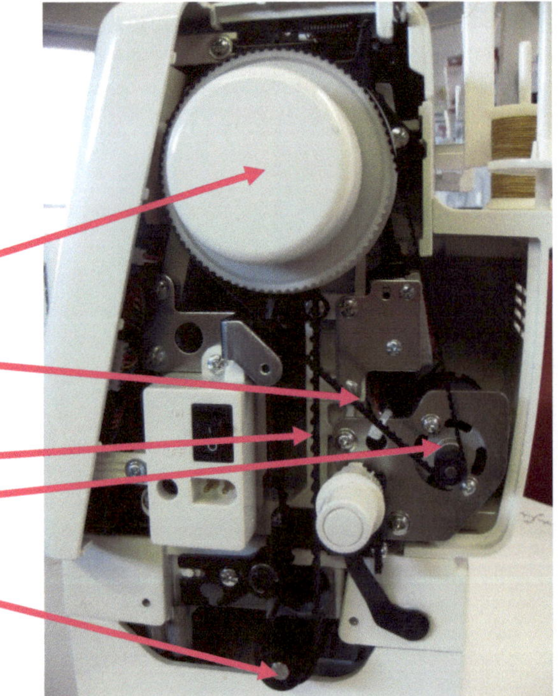

"It Won't Pick Up the Bobbin Thread"

Something I hear quite often when a machine comes in to the shop. We've discussed most of the causes in other places, but here they are again, this time in the same place.

First: Out of time. That'll do it for sure!
Second: Needle bent, or incorrectly installed.
Third: Bobbin case installed incorrectly.
Fourth: Incorrect needle/thread combination.
Fifth: Tail of thread out of the bobbin case too short. It may have been picked up, but was too short to get through the needle plate.

Generally speaking, anything that prevents the hook from picking up the loop at the back of the needle will generate this complaint. If you look at the list above, you'll see that, with the exception of the timing issue, these are all things you can fix at home at your sewing table.

"I Don't Get the Stitch I Selected"

If the machine is computerized, there may be a bad button, a bad connection at an internal cable, or a touch screen issue. The same comment applies to indicator lights that don't light when you select a feature that should cause them to light. If it's a button or a light, a circuit board may have to be replaced. These are pretty much all things for a technician to resolve.

If the machine is mechanical, with cams and followers, etc., then your machine probably needs service. Most of the selection issues with mechanical machines are gummed up and/or dry mechanisms. Fodder for your technician, as above.

I'll throw in an extra here. Most reverse (backstitch) problems with mechanical machines are from lack of service. They're just gummed up and dry.

-23-

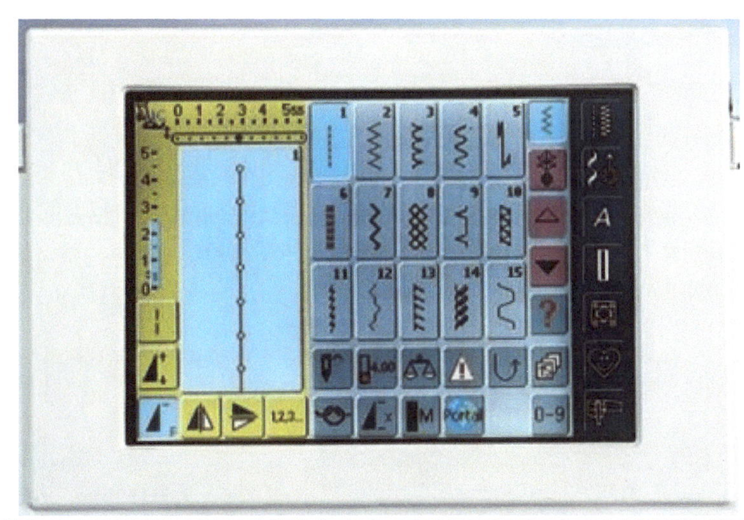

"My Machine Just Makes a Whirring Noise, and Won't Run"

The whirring noise is the bobbin winder on a machine with a separate motor to wind bobbins, and which doesn't have a button to start the winder, just the sensing arm. Someone bumped the arm and the machine thinks it's winding a bobbin. I've had people bring a machine in to the shop from long distances away, just for this problem. Definitely something you can take care of at home!

Another bobbin winder problem that will require a visit to your technician, is a winder that is extremely loud, and perhaps won't even wind anymore. Bobbin winders that don't use a separate motor for winding, (and that's most of them) use a rubber tire which is driven by the hand wheel. The rubber dries out and turns to stone after several years, and needs to be replaced. If your machine needle continues to go up and down, (ghosting), even after the bobbin winder clutch has been disengaged, it's time for service.

The other problem that generates this complaint, is a broken motor belt.

Thread Breakage

Surprisingly, I don't hear too many complaints about breaking thread. That's a good thing!

If you do experience this particular malady, however, there are some obvious things to check.:

One: Is the thread stifled in the needle groove? As we discussed in the needle section earlier, the cure
      is to change to a larger size needle.
Two: Check for burrs and nicks all along the thread path. If you find them, they can be polished out.
      That may be something a technician should do for you.
Three: If your machine is a very fast one, such as the new end loaders, and the thread you're using on
      the fine side, just slow down a bit.
Four: This one's not as obvious. Is your machine out of time? Make sure the fabric isn't still feeding
      when the needle pierces it.
Fifth: Is the thread getting tangled up as it comes off the spool, and before it gets to the first pre-tensioner?
Sixth: Are you using old cotton thread? Or really cheap thread? That's an obvious cure!

Walking Foot

(What's This Thing?)

A walking foot is a device to eliminate fabric bunching up ahead of the presser foot, usually when multiple fabric layers are being sewn. Sometimes it's a separate presser foot, sometimes it's built in to the machine itself.

It works by dropping extra feed dogs onto the fabric from the top. These upper feed dogs clamp the fabric from the top, and feed along with the regular lower feed dogs, so that the top and bottom fabric layers are equally fed. They work really well.

The complaint I hear from customers are that the add-on units are cumbersome, (somewhat true) and noisy. (also somewhat true) Those are minor problems, because the devices solve a major problem.

Bobbin Filling

We mentioned getting a birds nest in the bobbin after filling it in the bobbin section earlier. I see this fairly often, so it's worth another mention. It happens when the little round bobbin winder tension unit is missed when the machine is threaded to fill a bobbin. Bobbin tension (not bobbin case tension) is not critical, but it has to be there or the fill will be really bad.

Sometimes the bobbin will fill more at the bottom or top, giving it a cone shaped look. That can be corrected by raising or lowering the bobbin winder tension unit. You can give that a shot at home, or have a technician adjust it for you. If you can't get it in to a technician for a while, you can "help" it fill correctly by holding a pencil or other smooth round object in the thread path while the bobbin fills, and raising it or lowering it slightly to urge the thread to go where it doesn't want to.

Another problem with bobbin winding is too much thread on the bobbin, or not enough. This is also adjustable, but sometimes the adjustment is tricky and/or hidden away inside the machine. Not enough fill is a nuisance, too much fill will jam the bobbin inside the bobbin case, and that's a catastrophic event. If the adjustment is where you can see it, and you can intuitively understand how it works, give it a try; otherwise let a technician do it.

Squeaky Free Motion Foot

If your free motion (darning) foot is one with a vertical rod with a spring wrapped around the rod, squeaks are common. To take care of this at home, you will need a toothpick and some sewing machine oil. Using the toothpick, dip it in the oil, and then place the smallest drop of oil possible on the rod top and bottom, where it slides up and down inside the bracket that holds it. Then be sure to sew on some scrap fabric until the excess oil is gone. Another easy home fix, and a trip to the shop avoided.

The Needle Unthreads Itself

This happens on mechanical machines that don't stop with the needle up automatically when you stop sewing. They just coast to a stop randomly. That can put the take-up lever in a position where it can pull the thread right out of the needle when you start a new seam. The fix is easy; when you finish a seam, rotate the hand wheel (top towards you, always) until the take-up lever is just starting to go down. If you can't see the take-up lever on your particular machine, rotate the hand wheel until the needle just starts down. That'll take care of the problem.

Embroidery

With the exception of the feeding of the fabric, just about everything already covered applies to embroidery on a home machine.

Home embroidery machines come in two flavors: sewing and embroidery on the same machine, either with a built-in embroidery unit on a regular sewing machine, or an add-on embroidery unit for a regular machine, and dedicated embroidery machines, which have no built-in feed systems, and therefore can not be used as a sewing machine at all. The latter are popular with people who want to sew and embroider without a changeover situation. Makes sense if you have the space to have two machines set up at the same time, and, of course, the funds to purchase two machines.

The two problems I see as a technician with machine embroidery are thread handling between the spool and the first pre-tensioner, and inappropriate choices in stabilizers.

We've already discussed thread getting tangled up as a result of a twist in the thread as it comes off the end of the spool. Every embroidery machine I have seen takes the thread off the end of the spool. That's because thread is used much more rapidly, and in much larger quantities than in normal sewing. If your machine uses a horizontal thread delivery system, and tangling becomes an issue, the most reliable remedy is a thread stand behind the machine, which will have a vertical spool orientation, and will incorporate a longer thread path between the spool and the first pre-tensioner. Thread nets around each spool become a cumbersome remedy, because of multiple color changes. Spool stands are inexpensive and work quite well. If you are using very small (short) spools, and the thread is wrapping itself around the exposed end of the spool pin, try sliding the spool to the end of the spool pin, with two spool caps, one on each end of the spool. This is a problem you absolutely have to deal with, because it is a thread and needle breaker, and will ruin a project you are part way through should it occur.

Stabilizer choices are best made by consulting your local sewing machine dealer about your particular situation. There are many choices in stabilizers out there, and they should be able to advise you on your project.

Tension adjustment is important on embroidery machines, because of the large quantities of thread consumed in embroidery, and the cost of the thread. You don't want to be pulling large amounts of expensive top thread to the back of the stitches. If your machine is a "combo" machine, and sews as well as embroiders, you can set the tension in the sewing mode, using your embroidery thread, as we've already discussed. If the machine is a dedicated embroidery machine, you will have to hoop up a sample in order to check the tension.

If your machine has a removable embroidery unit, the unit shouldn't need service as often as your sewing machine. If it's built-in, it has to be serviced annually, as part of the machine service. If it's a dedicated machine, it needs service annually.

Transferring embroidery designs is a somewhat confusing area for lots of folks. And for good reasons!
Embroidery machines all come with built-in designs, but there are literally thousands of "after market/
third party" designs available, and people want to use them, as well they should.

The designs come in a variety of forms; early ones on a memory card, current ones on a CD or a flash
drive. Designs can be transferred from the purchased media with a variety of methods.
Some machines allow transfer directly from a CD through a dedicated CD reader, others require transferring from the purchased media to a flash drive, which can be inserted into the machine. Some provid-
ers furnish the media already on a flash drive. Some machines allow transfer directly from a personal
computer. If your machine only accepts memory cards, you probably are limited to purchasing designs
which are furnished on cards.

To further complicate matters, each manufacturer of embroidery machines has their own unique file for-
mat, which will be the only one that brand of machine will recognize. The purchased media will come
with the full spectrum of file formats, for that reason.
Generally, designs can be transferred from a CD to a flash drive directly in the embroidery machine, or
by copying and pasting in a computer to get the files on the flash drive.
With the proper software, you can actually digitize your own unique designs.

Most embroidery machines will choke on a flash drive that's too large, so try to use drives that are "2
GB" or less. Drives that small are getting hard to find, but are still available. Since embroidery designs
have small file sizes, you can put lots of designs on a small drive.

OK; got it? If you don't, you're in good company!

The machine manuals tend to gloss over this task, partly because they don't want to encourage after-
market buying, and partly because it's a complicated area and they want to avoid discouraging potential
buyers. (at least in my opinion)

Your best source of enlightenment is probably your local dealer, and/or technician. We all struggle with
this task, some more than others, but it can always be overcome! Because of the large amount of great
designs available, it's well worth the effort.

Glossary

Cams for Mechanical Machines

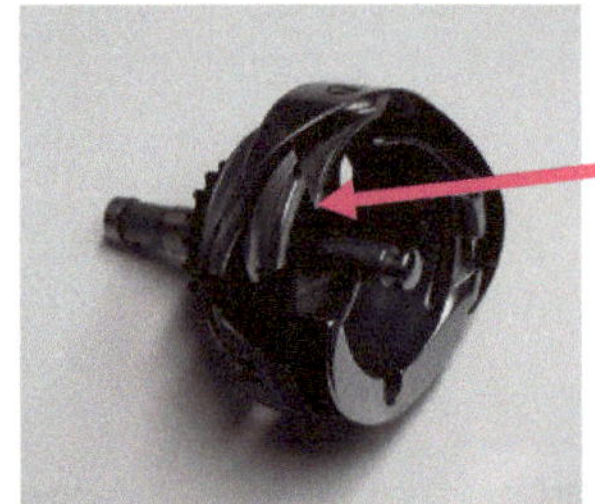

Camstack in the Machine

Hook Point

Oscillating Hook

Hook Point

Rotary Hook

Tension Adjustment Screw
Clockwise = Tighter
Counter Clockwise = Looser

Tension Spring

Front Loader Bobbin Case

Pull thread up through hole in bobbin, wind several layers, clip thread and finish winding bobbin.

Bobbin winding tension device.

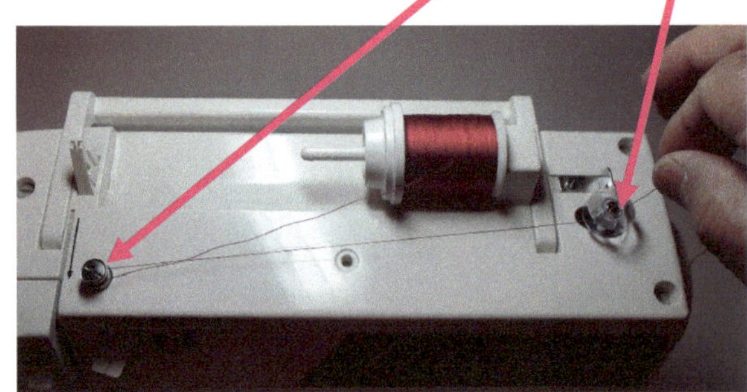

Bobbin Winding

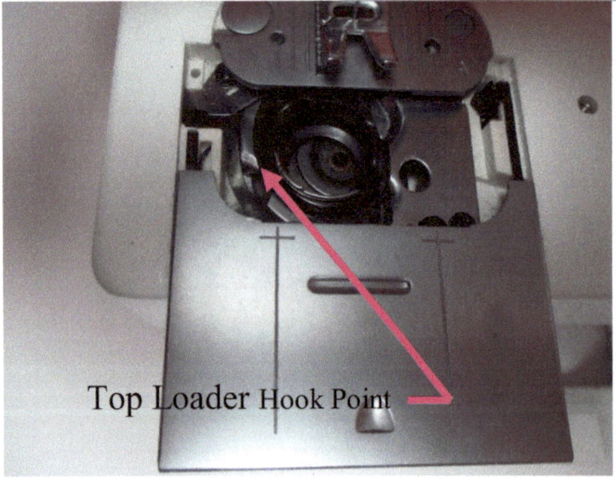

Top Loader Hook Point

Take Up Lever

Presser Foot Pressure

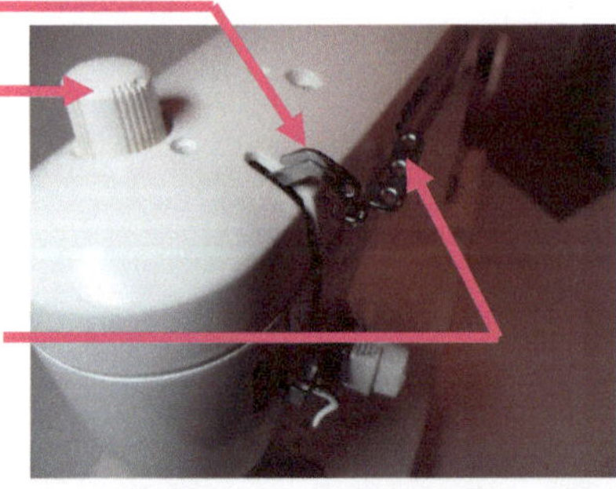

Blade Type Pre-tensioner

My Machine's Been Dropped!

No matter how careful we are, machines get dropped; off a cart, off the back of a truck, off the dining room table, by the movers, etc.

It's a fact, that unless it's in the factory packaging, shipping can result in the same sort of damage.

What I usually hear is that an un-named third party did it, but it doesn't matter at all who did it; it's going to be damaged! And a technician will have to asses the damage.

Should this happen to your baby, take a deep breath, relax, (sure!) and take the victim to a technician for an autopsy.

It's best not to turn the hand wheel or plug it in and try to run the machine, after a drop event, because internal parts get knocked about and may be in a position where other damage may occur if those parts are moved.

Because the center of gravity is toward the hand wheel end, machines quite often land on the hand wheel, which will push the upper shaft axially to where it's not supposed to be.

The good news is; most drop victims can be repaired, sometimes without even needing new parts!

Topic Index*

* This is not a comprehensive index, where every page that a word appears on is listed. I don't like those, and I'll bet you don't, either.

I've tried to list topics of interest, and the important pages that contribute to an understanding of that topic.

Some Final Thoughts

(Sometimes referred to as "Author's Notes")

Although I've tried to make the material presented here as simple as possible, the fact is that sewing machines are rather complicated critters. Much more so than one would expect.

If the text of this little piece is difficult for you to understand, and perhaps even somewhat boring, I apologize for that. Take from it whatever helps you, and don't worry too much about the stuff that doesn't make sense or that doesn't apply to your situation.

This material closely follows a verbal presentation I've been making over the years to quilt groups, customers and pretty much anyone who would listen. The feed-back from these presentations has been almost universally positive, so maybe there's some good stuff in here. I hope so.

If there's information in here that helps you avoid a service call, or that allows you to complete a promised project by it's due date, then it's served it's purpose.

When I've attended service training classes, (and there have been a bunch of those) I'm struck by the fact that the day to day problems my customers run into aren't the main thrust of the training. The training is needed, and always well presented, but it focuses on major repairs, and somehow misses the little everyday problems you face as a customer.

OK...I've been in trouble before, and probably will be again.

But I hope this helps you folks out there who need it the most!

Boone

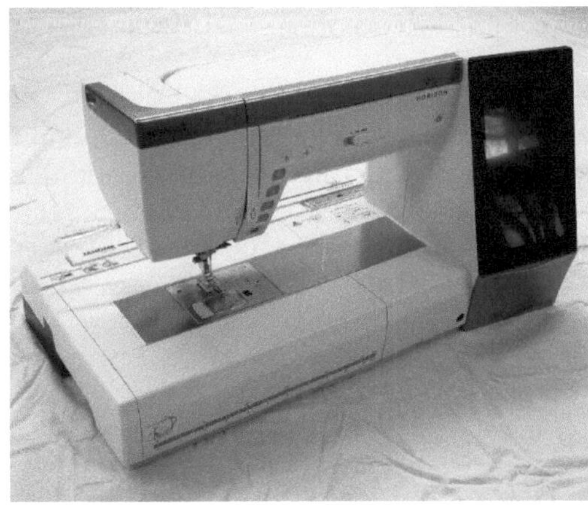

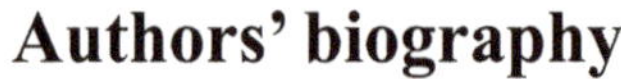Authors' biography

I was a Dustbowl/Depression baby, born in Amarillo, Texas, in 1933. A few years ago.
My family moved around quite a bit, and I've lived in several mid-western and western cities as well.

My education at Utah State University was interrupted by service in the U.S. Army. After the Army, where I was an instructor for tracked vehicle service and repair, (tanks) I earned a degree in Mechanical Engineering from USU. In 1959, if you're counting.

I met and married Viola while still studying at Utah State. We had two daughters, Kathleen and Christine, and a son, Gene, who are all grown up now. And a whole bunch of grandkids. Sadly, we lost Viola to Alzheimer's in 2010.

For the next 40 years, after graduation, I worked as an engineer for several companies, both large and small, and for myself as a consultant. My main specialty in those years was what's called "mechanism design." It actually encompassed many fields, including missile design for the Government, (rocket science?) and pretty much everything else, such as data processing equipment, medical devices, card readers, a very early design of a hard drive for data storing, printers of all sorts, finishing up in the late 1990s' with slot machine design. I hold several U.S. Patents. The oddest thing was probably designing a missile carrying box car for the ill-fated missile train. I don't think the train ever ran. Perhaps someone figured out that the bad guys could find the train by following the track.

The engineering business carried me to several overseas venues, and, as a result, I'm a well-seasoned world traveler.

I also spent a few of those years designing and building custom bicycles, mostly for racing. If you Google my name, what comes up are the bicycles.

I never designed a sewing machine, but did design a lot of similar mechanisms. I actually worked for Singer-Friden at one point, but not on sewing machines. I might still design one; it keeps tickling the back of my mind.

Current hobbies are sewing, building model railroads and square dancing. Earlier hobbies were race car building, cycling and running. I was somewhat younger for those.

All that design background comes in handy if you leave the world of retired design engineer and go back to work as a sewing machine technician, which I did, after the death of my wife. Long before she passed away, Viola got me interested in quilting, and that's been a continuous thing ever since. I guess because of their particular geometry, I'm drawn to Bargellos, and most of my quilts are of that type. Also, as a result of all those designing years, I can spot an engineering "band aid" in a sewing machine design from across the room!

I think I've enjoyed the sewing and the sewing machines as much as anything else I've done. I have no plans to stop. I'm still amazed that people are willing to pay me for having so much fun!

Boone

A place for notes.

(So you won't have sticky notes all over your machine)

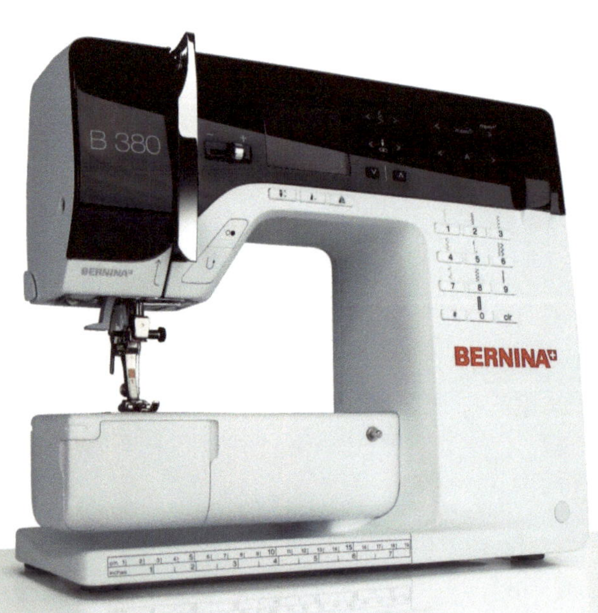

And More Notes !